Make Your Money Grow with Dividend Paying Stocks

By Doug West, Ph.D.

Make Your Money Grow with Dividend Paying Stocks

Copyright © 2016 Doug West

All Rights Reserved. No part of this book may be reproduced in any form without written permission from the author. Reviewers may quote brief passages in reviews.

Table of Contents

Preface v

Introduction vii

Chapter 1: What Are Stocks? 1

Chapter 2: How to Invest in Stocks 7

Chapter 3: How and Why Do Stock Prices Fluctuate? 9

Chapter 4: What Are Dividends? 15

Chapter 5: How to Invest in Dividends......................................21

Chapter 6: Dividends and Compound Interest 25

Chapter 7: What Factors Determine the Best Dividend Stocks? 29

Chapter 8: Best Stock Types for Dividends 35

Chapter 9: Dangers Associated with Dividend Investments....39

Chapter 10: Benefits of Dividend Stocks During Periods of Economic Downturn 43

Chapter 11: Diversification and Changing Markets.................49

Conclusion	51
Glossary	53
Further Reading	59
Internet Resources	60
Disclaimer	61
Acknowledgments	61
About the Author	63
Additional Books by Doug West	65
Index	67

Preface

Welcome to the book *Make Your Money Grow with Dividend Paying Stocks*. This book is part of the 30 Minute Book Series and, as the name of the series implies, if you are an average reader this book will take around 30 minutes to read. Since this book is not meant to be an all-encompassing book on investing in dividend paying stocks, you may want to know more about this subject. To help you with this, there are several good references at the end of this book. As you read through the book, if there are terms you are not familiar with, I have provided a Glossary of Terms at the end of the book that should help. Thank you for purchasing this book and I hope you enjoy it.

Doug West

June 2016

Introduction

Everyone dreams about making money without having to put in the work. While investing in stocks and making money through dividends does not come without some effort, it is a great way to take your savings nest egg and grow it to three or four times its current value. Relaxing at home and watching as the dividend checks roll in may seem as though it is a pipe dream, but this is reality for people who take the time to understand stocks and dividends.

The mistake a lot of people make with stocks and dividends is they desire to make a quick buck. While stocks and dividends do offer the possibility of significant gains in a short space of time, this type of strategy rarely translates to long-term success.

The purpose of this book is to guide the reader toward a path where they are making sustained progress toward their investment goals. While this method is not as glamorous as seeing your purchased stock's price rise by 300 or 400 percent in a few weeks, it is much less risky and more rewarding in the long run.

Buying stocks is considered the most important part of any investment portfolio. While you may also want to add other commodities or invest in bonds, making the right decisions with stock investments will make or break your attempts to grow your savings into a suitable retirement nest-egg.

There was a time when investing in stocks was limited to very wealthy individuals or major businesses. But thanks to the internet, everyone has the ability to gather information on the stock market. Not only can you get access to this information on a 24/7 basis, but you can also purchase stocks without having to invest thousands of dollars with a brokerage or mutual fund.

Even though the stock market is getting mainstream attention, most people still do not fully understand the best way to invest in stocks and dividends. Too many people rely on market trends, where flashy stocks are prioritized over solid and less glamorous picks. While those less glamorous stocks may not excite potential investors, they are the investment vehicles that will provide you with consistent dividends and proper growth over a 20 or 30-year period.

Instead of relying on hot tips from co-workers or "investment experts" on the internet, the best way to have sustained success in the stock market is to do your research, follow your instincts, and prioritize long-term success over short bursts of portfolio growth. While it is tempting to put a lot of money into stocks that are tipped to explode in the coming months and years, it is a dangerous policy that can backfire spectacularly.

Make Your Money Grow with Dividend Paying Stocks

Now we will explore the stock market from the ground up, with full explanations about stocks, how the stock market works, why stock prices rise and fall, how you can purchase stocks, and how you can benefit from stock dividends.

Chapter 1: What Are Stocks?

In simple terms, stocks are shares in a company that are sold to investors and the general public. When someone owns a stock, they own a certain percentage share in the company. Stockholders have a legal claim on a portion of the company's earnings and assets, which is proportional to how many stocks they own. For reference, the terms stocks, shares, and equity are interchangeable and have similar meanings.

Someone who owns stock in a company is one of the many owners of the business. People who own stocks are referred to as stockholders or shareholders. Even if someone owns a single stock in a major company, they are technically making a claim to a sliver of the company's assets and earnings. Not only do stockholders have a claim to the assets a company holds, but they also have a claim to any current or future earnings the company gains while they own the stock. Some stocks also come with voting rights, which allows stockholders to have a say in important decisions made by the company's CEO and/or board of directors.

When someone buys a stock, they are given a stock certificate. This piece of paper signifies that the individual owns a certain number of stocks in a company. While these papers still exist, most stock transactions are now done electronically. This not only eliminates a lot of the paperwork associated with owning stocks, but it also makes it easier to buy and sell stocks. In the past, stockholders would have to take their stock certificates to a brokerage in order to sell them. Now these transactions are completed online within minutes.

Stockholders must understand they are not going to have direct involvement in how companies are run on a day-to-day basis. Unless you own a significant amount of stock, such as a 50 or 60 percent share in the company, your involvement is restricted to voting on the company's board of directors at their annual shareholders' meetings. Similarly, stockholders are not entitled to walk up to a company's office at any time and demand a meeting with the company's CEO or CFO.

To illustrate the potential power of a stockholder, we will take an example where an investor owns 100 stocks of Company XYZ. If this fictitious company only has 500 total stocks, it means the investor owns one-fifth of the company, or 20 percent of all active shares. This share pool provides the investor with a significant ability to influence the company's policies through his voting rights. When there is an annual shareholders' meeting, the investor would vote in members to the board of directors who will follow his vision for the company.

In contrast, let us look at an example where the investor owns 100 stocks of Company XYZ, but in this scenario the company has 1,000,000 total shares. This means the investor owns 0.01 percent of the company's stock. Owning this much stock still gives him voting rights with regard to the board of directors, but his vote is only 0.01 percent of the total votes cast. With such little stock, the investor has almost no say in how the company will operate in the present and future.

But regular shareholders do not need to worry too much about their inability to influence a company's policies. These functions are performed by the millionaire and billionaire investors who buy up large portions of companies. A regular shareholder is much more interested in the company's stock price increasing, along with the possibility of receiving a share of the company's profits through dividend payments.

To reiterate, the major reason a person owns stock is to have a claim on the assets and earnings of a company. This is the one and only reason a regular investor would buy stocks in companies. Only investment firms and extremely wealthy individuals will buy stock with the purpose of influencing how a company is run in the future.

Since a stockholder owns a percentage of the assets and earnings in a company, is it not logical that they would also share in the company's liabilities? Wrong. Stockholders have limited liability, which means they are not personally liable in the event that a company cannot pay back the debts it owes. The only amount of money a stockholder can lose is the amount of money they spent to buy those stocks.

For example, let us continue with the same investor and say that he spent $10 each on his 100 shares in Company XYZ. If Company XYZ is deep in debt and ceases to exist, the investor is only going to lose the $1000 he spent to buy those 100 shares, since Company XYZ's stock price will likely tank. No one is legally allowed to come after the investor, or other shareholders, to seek money Company XYZ owed at the time of its demise.

Now we have a better understanding of stocks, but we must also understand why companies are issuing stock. What do companies such as Apple and Microsoft gain from issuing stocks to investors? Is it not better for the company's owners to keep all the company's assets and earnings to themselves? Why share this money with thousands of strangers, who might have an influence on how the company operates?

Companies sell stock because they want to raise money. There are many ways to raise money, such as borrowing from banks or financial institutions. But the most popular way for companies to raise money is through share issuances. By issuing stock, the company gains a significant amount of money that they never have to pay back. While many companies will issue dividends to investors when they make profits, these dividends are never comparable in value to the money a company gets from stock issuance.

So why are stockholders accepting these terms? Why do they let companies make all this money through stock issuances when they know the company will never pay back the money? Because they are buying stocks in the hope that the stock's price will rise over time.

If our investor bought the 100 shares in Company XYZ for $10 each at the time of Company XYZ's stock issuance, he is hoping that Company XYZ's stock will double or triple in value over time. This will allow the investor to eventually sell the stock and make a profit on his initial investment.

But this deal does not come without risks. There are absolutely no guarantees when it comes to buying company stocks. Even if you are investing in the most reputable and famous company in the world, there is a risk this company could begin to struggle at any time. Companies have no obligation to share their profits with investors through dividends, and there is no way for investors to make back the money they lose if a stock's price tanks because the company makes bad decisions.

This is why a lot of stock market novices end up crashing and burning. They will start out by purchasing flashy stocks that they think will triple or quadruple in value. But instead of diversifying their investments and putting the bulk of their money in reliable stocks, they invest too much money in these up and coming companies. When the company goes under, the investor loses their money because the company's stock is now worth nothing.

It is up to each individual investor to balance the risk involved in stock market investments with the potential rewards of stock price increases and dividends. This is why the right investment strategy is so important.

Chapter 2: How to Invest in Stocks

Many people want to invest in the stock market, but they are always dissuaded by the misguided notion that it requires thousands of dollars to make an initial investment in the market. While there was a time when stock market investment meant having thousands of dollars in your savings account, it is now possible to start venturing into the market with much less money.

The two main ways to invest in the stock market are through Direct Investment Plans or brokerages. Direct Investment Plans are plans where people can buy a company's stock directly through the company. But there is typically a minimum value of stock a person must purchase. Most Direct Investment Plans will require between $100 to $500 of minimum investment. If someone only has $1,000 they want to invest in the market, being limited to investments in two or three companies is not ideal—but it is a good start.

This is why most people prefer dealing with brokerages. Now there are two major types of brokerages: full service brokerages and discount brokerages. A full service brokerage will provide a lot more assistance to a beginning investor, but they also require investments of at least $40,000 or $50,000. They have full time employees who manage the investor's money in the right manner, but this means you need a lot more money up-front in order to garner the interest of a full service brokerage.

Small time investors are left with only one realistic option: discount brokerages. Thanks to the internet, discount brokerages are easily found and not difficult to rate. Entities such as OptionsHouse, Merrill Edge, Robinhood, Loyal3, and eTrade are examples of discount brokerages where investors can buy stocks without having to make huge investments.

Chapter 3: How and Why Do Stock Prices Fluctuate?

If you ever spent time analyzing stock prices or general market trends, you would notice that stock prices are changing every single day. In fact, most stocks will fluctuate in price on a minute-by-minute basis. These prices are shifting because of the supply and demand for these stocks. If there is greater demand for a stock as compared to the supply, its price increases. In contrast, limited demand for a stock combined with increased supply will result in the price dropping.

But this part is often the easiest to understand. Supply and demand is taught in high school economics, and its principles most certainly apply to the stock market. However, individuals often have a harder time understanding why investors may like a particular stock and dislike another. Analyzing market trends and predicting stock performance is all about understanding how news is grouped. Where stocks are concerned, investors must know what news is considered positive and what is considered negative.

Problems with this strategy arise because different types of investors have different ideas about how positive and negative news is defined. For example, a company could release their earnings report for the year and have it interpreted completely differently by three unique investors. One investor will consider the earnings report indicative of the company's strength, while another will analyze it as a sign that the company is beginning to falter. The third investor may view the news as neither negative nor positive.

Each of these investors will react differently to the news as well. The first investor will consider buying the company's stock, while the second investor may sell. Since the third investor is neutral on the news, they will probably have no reaction to this news. If they already own the company's stock, they will not sell. But if they are not a current shareholder, the news will not tempt them to buy into the company either.

Despite the propensity for differing reactions among investors, we can analyze some theories of stock price movements. A good way to look at the movement of a company's stock is by equating it with the market's overall worth of a company. If investors feel a company is worthwhile, they are more likely to want its stock. If they do not believe it's worthwhile, they are more likely to sell its stock.

People often make the mistake of equating stock price with a company's value. The value of a company, or its market capitalization, is the stock price multiplied by the number of outstanding shares. Beginning investors may look at two companies and determine the one with a higher stock price also has a higher value. But they may be wrong.

For example, let's say Company A has a stock price of $100 and 100 outstanding shares. This puts its value at $10,000. Now we look at a Company B, which has a price of $75 but 1000 outstanding shares. This company has a value of $75,000. While Company A has the higher share price, it has a significantly lower value than Company B. But investors are more excited by the worth and potential of Company A, which is why it has a higher share price.

What impacts a company's value? The primary factor is the company's earnings. If a company is not making a profit in the long run, it will not survive. Companies that cannot make money during a sustained period of time will not stay in business. But this does not mean a company going through a couple of years with minimal profits is doomed. This is why investors often consider more than the short term earnings when they make buying or selling decisions regarding company stock.

Companies listed on the stock exchange are legally bound to report their earnings on a quarterly basis, which is why there are often news articles about a particular company's earnings report. Analysts and investors will often base their buying and selling decisions on these earnings reports. But they are not only looking at the actual earnings, but the comparison of the earnings with the projected earnings.

For example, a company may have spent a lot of money in a quarter in order to grow the business. This means they are anticipating low earnings, which was already mentioned in their previous report. If the earnings in their latest report are in line with those expectations, investors will not react negatively to the news. But if the earnings are much worse than anticipated, it will raise alarm bells and prompt some investors to sell the company's stock.

In contrast, a company that reports better-than-expected earnings will receive a boost through its stock price. More investors will want to purchase the company's stock, because they see it as being on an upward trajectory.

But earnings are not the only factors that influence stock market decisions. For example, we can look at the dot com bubble of the early 2000s to understand how companies with limited profits can still prompt incredible excitement from investors. In many cases, these companies raised excitement because of their potential for huge earnings in the future.

In reality, many people believe that it is almost impossible to predict stock prices with any degree of certainty. While the real world performance of companies plays a major role in how their stocks are priced, these prices are similarly impacted by the feelings, expectations, and predictions of investors. This is why there are so many stories of companies and entire industries going through periods of boom, where the stock price rose exponentially, only to suffer dramatic crashes later.

This is why the best tool available to investors in terms of market analysis is the historic performance of companies and market sectors. It is also the reason the rest of this book focuses on the importance of dividends. Instead of delving too deep into playing the stock market, we look at the importance of selecting stocks that have displayed consistent performance over the past 20 to 30 years.

Chapter 4: What Are Dividends?

Dividends are part of a company's quarterly or yearly earnings. They are given out on a cyclical basis to certain types of shareholders. The amount and frequency of dividends given out by a particular company is determined by the company's board of directors. These dividends are typically given out by companies as cash, stock shares, or other types of investments.

Companies have a number of choices available to them when they report a profit for a given quarter. They can keep the profits for themselves, which is referred to as retained earnings. This is often what happens with newer companies that are still trying to establish their market presence. A company also has the option of investing their earnings into further expansions, market research, advertising, or the development of other departments. The third option available to a business is to give their earnings to shareholders as dividends.

Some companies will also conduct share buybacks through their net profits, which is a method of buying their own stock from stockholders in the open market. However, these buybacks do not impact the company's stock in the same way the stock prices fluctuate when investors buy or sell the company's stock. A company will engage in share buybacks if they find their company is undervalued. They may also find their company is a much better investment than anything else on the market.

Dividends are not only paid out by major companies, but also by mutual funds and ETFs. If an investor or organization owns stocks in these mutual funds or ETFs, they receive dividends when the fund makes a profit.

Mutual funds are investment vehicles where money is collected from a number of individuals or businesses. The people in charge of the mutual fund will use this money to invest in stocks, bonds, or other assets, with a view to growing each individual investor's pool of money.

Exchange-Traded Funds, or ETFs, are market securities that track particular indexes, commodities, bonds, or groups of assets. Unlike a mutual fund, the ETF will trade on the stock exchange like a common company stock.

With these mutual funds and ETFs, shareholders and investors can also receive a capital gain distribution. This form of dividend arises from situations where fund managers liquidate profitable assets within their mutual fund. The profits from these liquidations are split among the mutual fund or ETF's shareholders.

Now that we understand the purpose of dividends, it is important for potential investors to note how these dividends are distributed by companies. There is a specific process where a company decides whether they will issue dividends and when shareholders can expect to redeem these dividends.

The declaration date is a specific date where the payment of dividends is announced by the board of directors of a company. On the declaration date, the board of directors provide a statement that refers to the dividend's declaration date, the size of the dividend, the record date, the ex-dividend date, and the date of payment.

To better illustrate this point, we can take a hypothetical example where the company releases information about the dividend on the first of the month, which also happens to be a Monday. This means the first of the month is the declaration date. The statement will set a record date and an ex-dividend date. The record date is the day when the company browses their electronic records and makes a list of the shareholders who are owed dividends. This is typically a few days to a week after the declaration date. In our example, the record date may be the fifth of the same month.

The ex-dividend date is always three days before the record date, and this is the last day investors may buy shares in the company to become eligible for dividends from that quarter. In our example, the ex-dividend date is the second of the month. Investors would then have until the second to purchase the shares and receive dividends on those same shares. Investors who buy shares after May 2 would not receive dividends for that period, because they did not meet the ex-dividend date.

The reason investors must buy their stocks three days before the ex-record date is because this is the amount of time it takes for all the paperwork and behind-the-scenes work of a stock purchase to reach completion. An individual is not formally the owner of stock until three days pass from the date of their purchase.

Now we come to the payment date, which is the date when the dividends are paid out to investors. This usually happens between a week to ten days after the ex-record date. The payment date for dividends is usually a week or ten days after the record date. In our example, dividends are paid out anywhere from the 12th to 15th of the same month.

The final part regarding the concept of dividends pertains to the analysis of a company's dividend payments. Investors use many tools to analyze dividend payments, such as the dividend rate, dividend yield, and payout ratio.

The dividend rate is a method of calculating all the annualized dividend payments an investor gets from the stock they own. This includes regular dividend payments along with non-recurring payments during this period. The dividend rate is calculated with the following simple formula:

Dividend Rate = (Recurring Dividend) * (Number of Dividend

Periods in the Year) + Non-Recurring Dividends

Some companies have fixed dividend rates, while others have adjustable rates. We can look at an example where a company pays a $10 dividend on a quarterly basis, along with an annual bonus dividend of $2 per share because of a particularly profitable event that they did not expect. In this case, the Dividend Rate = ($10) * (4) + $2 = $42.

Another tool of analysis is the dividend yield, which is a way for investors to understand how much money a company is paying out to their investors relative to share price. The dividend yield is a percentage and it is calculated by dividing the annual dividends per share by the price per share. This is a great way for investors to understand the "bang for their buck" of their stock investments.

We can use a hypothetical example to understand dividend yield:

Company A had their most recent dividend payout at $2 per share. At the time, their share price was around $60. This means the dividend yield on the Company A stock was at 3.33%.

While our example is entirely hypothetical, a dividend yield of between two to ten percent is a fairly common number for stable companies. While they do pay out dividends on stocks on a regular basis, they do not pay a huge amount. Their focus is on improving their brand, investing in new technologies and products, and ensuring they are providing consistently solid dividends to their investors.

The final analysis tool is the payout ratio, which is a way to define the percentage of a company's earnings that are being given to shareholders through dividends. We calculate the payout ratio by dividing the dividends per share by the earnings per share. For example, a hypothetical company that offers $10 in dividends per share and earns $40 per share has a payout ratio of 25 percent.

Chapter 5: How to Invest in Dividends

Understanding the concept of dividends is a key tool for those who are determined to succeed in the long-term with their investment strategy. In terms of how to invest in dividends, it is as simple as purchasing stocks in companies that are offering dividends. It is important for investors to complete their research, because it is never a good idea to assume a company will continue to offer dividends.

Many companies have a policy where they do not offer any dividends, because they are more concerned with growing their business and establishing a dominant position in their given market or industry. Meanwhile, other companies are overly focused on dividends, which means they neglect to keep enough of their earnings to offset a potentially bad quarter or year.

For this reason, it is crucial for investors to find the right balance with their dividend investments. While you do not want to spend thousands of dollars in stocks of companies that do not offer dividends, you also want to avoid companies that jeopardize their long-term health for the short-term satisfaction of offering high dividends to investors.

Aside from buying stocks and receiving cash dividends on a quarterly basis, investors can also participate in Dividend Reinvestment Plans, or Dividend Reinvestment Programs. These programs are a fantastic tool for investors, because they allow for the possibility of purchasing new stock from the money provided by a company as dividends.

For example, let us say that Company XYZ offers their investors the opportunity to participate in a Dividend Reinvestment Program. This means an investor can use the money provided by Company XYZ as dividend to buy more stocks in Company XYZ. Instead of pulling out the money and placing it in your bank as liquid cash, you are using the same money to invest more money in the company in hopes of getting a better return on your investment.

The structure of a Dividend Reinvestment Plan is fairly simple. When investors get regular dividends, they typically arrive in the mail as a check or in your bank account as a direct deposit. If someone enrolls in the Dividend Reinvestment Plan, they no longer get these checks or direct deposits. The dividend money is automatically used to buy more shares of the company's stock at its current average market price.

The reason many investors go with these plans is because of how easy it is to sign up and reap the rewards. The process is completely automated and requires little more than a quarterly confirmation from the investor to make sure everything is going smoothly.

There are minimal fees attached with participating in these plans, while some companies offer the plans without any fees at all. And the best part is that an investor can purchase fractional shares through the plans, which means they get a percentage of a share if the dividend payment in a given quarter is not enough to buy a full share in the company. Some programs even offer investors the option of making a cash payment, in order to purchase additional shares. These payments can range from $25 to $100, depending on how many shares the investor wants.

This is a low-cost way of buying more shares in a company, because you are avoiding the fees and commissions associated with the discount brokerages mentioned in the earlier chapters. While the fees with discount brokerages are minimal, it is still cheaper to use the optional cash payment method to buy additional stock in a company that is providing you with consistent dividends on a quarterly basis.

Chapter 6: Dividends and Compound Interest

One of the key reasons investors will participate in Dividend Reinvestment Programs or Plans is because of the concept of compound interest and how it impacts returns from stock and dividend investments. When we talk about compound interest, we are referring to the practice of calculating interest on the principal balance along with the accumulated interest from the previous periods.

In order to better explain this concept, we will use a hypothetical example. In this example, we have a principal amount of money of $2,000. The interest rate in our example is 10 percent, while the time period is ten years. Thanks to the magic of compound interest, we will end the ten-year period with a total interest amount of $3,187. Adding it to the original amount, we are left with $5,187 on our initial $2,000 investment after ten years.

While we can see this is a fairly substantial amount, you can only properly understand the wonders of compound interest by comparing the amount to a situation where interest rates are not compounded. We will use the numbers from the above example, where an investor puts in $2,000 and the annual interest rate is 10 percent. After a ten-year period, the investor would earn

$2,000 in interest, which takes the total amount to $4,000. This is a loss of $1,187 over ten years because of a lack of compounding interest.

And the biggest reason to consider compound interest investments is because your potential gains will only increase as your investment amount increases. If the hypothetical investor mentioned above had invested $20,000 instead of $2,000, the difference in his earnings between compounding and regular interest would have been much higher.

But how does compound interest apply to dividends and stock market investments?

For investors who invest in companies that offer dividends, there is the possibility of reinvesting this dividend money back into the market. As mentioned in the previous chapter, this is possible through Dividend Reinvestment Plans. By enrolling in one of these plans, the investor is compounding their earnings because they are earning more money through this reinvestment then they would if they had taken the money and put it in their checking or savings account.

To understand the impact of compounding on dividend profits, we will take an example where someone invests $30,000 in a stock that offers dividends. This stock offers a 10 percent annual return. If someone kept reinvesting the money they earned from dividends into the same dividend-offering stock at that annual return rate for 10 years, they would have $77,812.

In comparison, if the investor in the above example only invested the original $30,000 in the dividend stock, and simply deposited the yearly dividends in a checking account with next to no interest, they would only end up with $30,000 in dividend payments after ten years, plus the original $30,000 of company stock. They would have a total of $60,000, which is a loss of $17,812.

This example highlights the potential benefits of reinvesting dividends and using the principles of compound interest. But investors must remember that there are risks with this type of investment, because you are continuously putting the money you earn from dividends back in the stock market. There is always the risk of a profitable and reputable company going through a bad spell, which hurts their stock price. In this case, the investor would not only stop receiving dividends, but they could lose a substantial amount of their money because of the drop in the company's share price. If you are going to participate in dividend reinvestments, it is absolutely crucial that you choose the right companies.

Chapter 7: What Factors Determine the Best Dividend Stocks?

There are some investors who seek significant increases in their investment money by placing their money in high dividend yield stocks. There are plenty of stocks trading on the market that offer substantial dividends, with some having a payout ratio of greater than 0.50 or 50 percent. However, these stocks can be risky, for the simple reason that they are giving up a huge portion of the money they earn to their investors through dividends.

When comparing high dividend yield stocks to major, stable company stocks, we can analyze that a few bad quarters could destroy the entire business of a high dividend yield stock. This is in sharp contrast to companies such as Microsoft and Apple, because they keep a large chunk of their money within the company to offset against such risks.

A company or fund that is paying out more than half its profits as dividends has much less wiggle room. If something goes wrong for this company, they are going to struggle. This is why investors must think very carefully before investing in companies with such a high rate of paying out dividends.

Despite the risks associated with stock investment, there are many successful companies that have been paying dividends to their investors for years, while maintaining a payout ratio of between 0.35 to 0.55. Examples of these companies include Verizon Communications and General Motors. Verizon had a 51 percent payout ratio in the past year.

Verizon Communications Inc. (VZ) - NYSE ★ Watchlist
50.62 ↑0.46(0.92%) May 27, 4:03PM EDT

Prev Close:	50.16	Day's Range:	50.18 - 50.86
Open:	50.39	52wk Range:	38.06 - 54.49
Bid:	50.66 x 100	Volume:	10,649,467
Ask:	50.68 x 400	Avg Vol (3m):	13,153,300
1y Target Est:	52.26	Market Cap:	206.34B
Beta:	0.460456	P/E (ttm):	11.48
Next Earnings Date:	26-Jul-16	EPS (ttm):	4.41
		Div & Yield:	2.26 (4.46%)

Figure – Verizon Communications Stock Information (courtesy Yahoo finance, 5/27/2016)

An analysis of Verizon Communications indicates that it is one of the best stocks an investor can choose if they are looking for a steady and profit-generating investment. The company boasts a very high, consistent and gradually increasing yearly revenue. They also offer stable dividends, with the 2011 to 2015 dividends at 1.98, 2.03, 2.09, 2.16, and 2.23, respectively.

During the same years, Verizon had an earnings-per-share of 4.37, 2.42, 4, 0.31, and 0.85, respectively. This indicates that Verizon is fully committed to providing their investors with increasing dividends, even if the company happens to have a disappointing earnings year.

The reason they can get away with this strategy is because of the huge revenue they earn every year, along with the stability of their business. While companies going for a high dividend yield strategy can suffer after bad years, Verizon has such a major role in many diffcrent communications fields that their staying power is tremendous.

When analyzing the company's payout ratio, we see that Verizon sits at 0.51, 0.89, 0.52, 6.55, and 2.32 for the time period from 2011 to 2015. The company's price-to-earnings ratio hovered between 30 to 40 in 2011 and 2012. The Verizon price-to-earnings ratio climbed significantly in the first two quarters of 2013, because of their relatively poor earnings in 2011 and 2012. Since the start of 2014, it has hovered between 10 to 20.

The price-to-earnings, or P/E, ratio is a calculation of the price per share divided by the earnings-per-share from the last four quarters. For example, a company that trades at $10 per share with an earnings-per-share of $2 would have a P/E ratio of 5.

It is also important to remember that the P/E ratio of a company at any given time reflects the previous four quarters' worth of data. Companies that have a high price/earnings ratio are displaying a high stock price despite their modest earnings per share.

When a company has a high P/E ratio, it is telling us that investors believe they are going to experience significant growth over the coming years. In the case of Verizon Communications, investors were correct. Their earnings per share rose significantly in 2013 and 2015.

Verizon ticks all the boxes when it comes to solid investments. But what are investors looking for when they are selecting the best stocks for dividends? The three most important features of a solid dividend-paying stock are a reasonable P/E ratio, a solid payout ratio, and a tradition of paying steady dividends to investors.

If a company has a high Price-Earnings Ratio, investors are anticipating high earnings in the coming quarters and years. If the P/E ratio is very low, there are two possible meanings. Either the company is extremely undervalued or it is performing much better than it was in the past few years. By itself, the P/E ratio is not a perfect way to understand whether a company is worthy of your investment. But it is possible to look at a company's P/E ratio over a period of time and compare it to the average P/E ratio for the industry.

Another metric for measuring a company's value is through the payout ratio. This is calculated by taking the dividends per share and dividing them by earnings per share.

With the P/E ratio and the payout ratio, it is important to trust companies that have steady values. While you do not want to invest your money in companies with low ratios, it is also a good idea to avoid companies that have very high P/E or payout ratios. This is especially true for the payout ratio, because companies that are giving out more than 50 or 60 percent of their earnings for each share in dividends may display extreme volatility with respect to their stock price.

When looking for the best stocks to buy for the purpose of receiving dividends, look for companies that historically provide steady dividends to investors. Ultimately, you are not going to double your money in a few years through dividend investments. The purpose of this investment strategy is to see significant returns over the long term, which means you must prioritize companies that consistently pay out dividends for twenty or thirty years in a row. It is these companies that will provide you with the most value down the road, not companies that have exciting payout ratios of 90 percent over a period of a few years.

Chapter 8: Best Stock Types for Dividends

Whenever someone asks investors about the types of stocks that pay out the most dividends on a consistent level, they will begin to talk about companies in the telecommunications and utilities sectors. On average, telecommunications companies offer 5 percent yields and companies in the utilities sector offer 3.5 percent yields. A stock's yield is referring to the income generated from an investment.

The companies that are paying dividends on a consistent basis are not always the companies that have the highest percentage increases in dividend payments on an annual basis. These companies, which are usually in the telecoms and utilities sectors, are focused on remaining consistent with their long term goals for the company and with their dividend payments to investors.

As highlighted in an earlier chapter with the example of Verizon Wireless, consistently increasing dividend payments are expected when you invest in these companies. However, you are unlikely to see dividend percentage increases of 20 or 30 percent per year from companies in the telecoms or utilities industry.

People who are looking for those types of jumps can turn their attention to consumer discretionary or financials stocks. These sectors offer the best percentage increase from one year to another, but the companies in these sectors are also unpredictable in terms of their stock price. A great few years may be followed by a very poor year, which makes them a tougher sell as long term investments. The dividends may be great for one or two years, but bad news about the company's earnings could result in a significant stock price decline.

When considering stock types for dividends, always look at consumer staples as a good indicator for larger companies that will always remain on solid footing regardless of how the economy is performing. Consumer staples are goods that people will not eliminate from their budget, even if they are making much less money than before. Companies such as Coca-Cola and Phillip Morris are in the business of consumer staples.

The table below lists twelve companies that have a long history of paying a respectable dividend. By no means are these the only companies worth considering for your portfolio. At the end of the book is a section called "Internet Resources," which links the go-to websites that will help you identify companies you may want to invest in. These websites provide a lot of current information about companies, the business climate, and the economy, and they point to stocks to avoid, and stocks to consider for your dividend portfolio.

Company	Symbol	Sector	P/E	Pay Out Ratio	Dividend Yield (%)
AT&T, Inc.	T	Communications	16.52	0.81	4.94
Coca-Cola Company	KO	Consumer	26.96	0.84	3.13
Consolidated Edison	ED	Utility	18.94	0.70	3.58
Johnson & Johnson	JNJ	Health	20.61	0.58	2.83
McDonald's Corp.	MCD	Restaurant	23.68	0.68	2.88
Philip Morris Intl.	PM	Consumer	23.39	0.96	4.12
Realty Income Co.	O	REIT	56.03	2.23	3.99
Southern Company	SO	Utility	19.21	0.88	4.66
The Clorox Company	CLX	Consumer	25.34	0.63	2.47
Verizon Communications	VZ	Communications	11.48	0.51	4.51
Walgreens Boots	WBA	Consumer	25.12	0.47	1.88
Walmart Stores	WMT	Consumer	15.64	0.44	2.82

Table – 12 Dividend Paying Stock with Long Track Records as of 5/27/2016

Chapter 9: Dangers Associated with Dividend Investments

Having touched on the types of dividend stocks an investor should purchase, it is also important to look at some of the dangers associated with buying stocks for the purposes of getting dividends. There are many companies that offer significant dividends on a quarterly basis, which makes them attractive to new investors. But there are dangers associated with some of these companies that every investor must understand before they make a stock purchase.

A number of companies with very high dividend payments are attempting to sway investors through this method. They want investors to ignore the company's earnings report and focus on the huge dividends they are getting. These companies are often in distress, which means the dividends may not be so enticing in a couple of quarters. When the general market gets wind of the company's problems, the stock price could also tank, which means the investor not only stops getting dividends but also loses a significant chunk of their initial investment.

There are also cases where companies have a temporarily high dividend yield because their stock price tanked over the past few weeks or months. For example, Company A originally had a stock price of $100 and a dividend of $5, giving it a dividend yield of 5 percent. If the stock price plummeted to $50 because of some bad earnings report news, but the company continued to provide the same level of dividends to entice investors, the dividend yield is now 10 percent.

If a novice investor sees the 10 percent dividend yield and respectable share price, they could be forgiven for thinking the company is a solid investment. But if this company is on a downward trajectory, their poor earnings will eventually force them to stop giving out dividends. They might also experience further decreases in share price.

Too many new investors who get caught up in the concept of dividends forget to think about the important role of share price in their overall investment. While dividend payments over time are great, it is ultimately a company's share price that determines the overall success of your investment.

For example, Company B may have a dividend yield of 15 percent for the year. But if Company B's stock price dropped by 35 percent, the investor is definitely losing money overall. It is very important to tally up the risk of a company's share price declining with the upside of receiving higher dividends. Finding the right balance will provide the most stable and secure long-term investments for dividend seekers.

Another minor risk of focusing too much on dividend payments in your investment portfolio is that many of these stocks do not rise significantly when the market booms. When we talk about the best stock investments for dividend purposes, we must also mention that a number of these companies do not get massive share price spikes when the market has a great year. Their share price will go up, but not as much as some other, more volatile stocks.

It is up to the individual investor to find the balance between long-term investments that pay steady dividends and only see modest share price rises, and those investments that can provide a short-term boost during times of economic boom.

Chapter 10: Benefits of Dividend Stocks During Periods of Economic Downturn

Many investors look at the economy in a cyclical way. For every massive bubble and boom there is an inevitable bursting of the bubble and subsequent bust. But there are ways to mitigate against the risk associated with market troubles. Investors spend too much time focusing on trendy stocks that will rise and fall with the general economy, when they should pay more attention to quality dividend stocks. Many of these companies offer overall market beating returns, which is why they are so popular among long-term investors.

The only downside to some of these companies is that they may not rise with the same intensity as the rest of the market when we are experiencing a boom. But this is not a huge problem for long-term investors who are looking for consistent returns, as opposed to a get rich quick scheme. These businesses are able to pay steadily rising dividends to their investors no matter how their company or the overall market is performing. Some of these businesses will even post increasing profits during periods of economic recession.

The Clorox Company (CLX) - NYSE ★ Watchlist			
129.70 ↑0.16 (0.12%) May 27, 4:02PM EDT			
Prev Close:	129.54	Day's Range:	129.29 - 130.09
Open:	129.86	52wk Range:	103.77 - 133.24
Bid:	129.65 x 700	Volume:	481,413
Ask:	129.68 x 200	Avg Vol (3m):	1,107,700
1y Target Est:	124.67	Market Cap:	16.78B
Beta:	0.322707	P/E (ttm):	25.34
Earnings Date:	Aug 1 - Aug 5 (Est.)	EPS (ttm):	5.12
		Div & Yield:	3.20 (2.47%)

Figure – Clorox Stock Information (courtesy Yahoo Finance, 5/27/2016)

To better understand the effects of a market downturn on quality dividend stocks, we now take a look at three such stocks. The first company to analyze is Clorox, which produces consumer goods and has a market cap of roughly $16.8 billion. This is the conglomerate behind brands you will often see on the shelves at major stores, such as Clorox, Pine-Sol, Brita filters, Glad, and Hidden Valley. If there is a major and reliable consumer brand good on the shelves, there is a good chance it falls under the Clorox conglomerate.

With an incredible record of paying increasing dividends for the past 38 years, Clorox is one of the best stocks to purchase if you are looking for a reliable long-term investment that also provides the option to reinvest dividend returns. The reason this company performs so well in recessions is because most of its products are staple household items that people need whether they are in a good financial situation or a bad one.

Looking at the performance of Clorox during the recession, it is interesting to see that their earnings-per-share increased from 2007 to 2008 from $3.23 to $3.24 to $3.81.

Another company with similarly impressive results is Johnson & Johnson, which has been giving its investors increasing dividends for 53 straight years! Over the past 31 years, Johnson & Johnson has an adjusted growth when measuring the earnings-per-share. This increase continued during the economic recession, where Johnson & Johnson posted earnings-per-share growth from $4.15 in 2007 to $4.57 in 2008 and $4.63 in 2009.

Johnson & Johnson (JNJ) - NYSE ★ Watchlist
113.06 ↑0.16(0.14%) May 27, 4:00PM EDT

Prev Close:	112.90	Day's Range:	112.69 - 113.34
Open:	113.04	52wk Range:	81.79 - 115.00
Bid:	113.06 x 100	Volume:	4,647,024
Ask:	113.17 x 300	Avg Vol (3m):	7,376,100
1y Target Est:	117.44	Market Cap:	310.99B
Beta:	0.788333	P/E (ttm):	20.61
Earnings Date:	Jul 12 - Jul 18 (Est.)	EPS (ttm):	5.49
		Div & Yield:	3.20 (2.83%)

Figure – Johnson & Johnson Stock Information
(courtesy Yahoo Finance, 5/27/2016)

Interesting, the maximum drawdown of Johnson & Johnson during the recession reached almost 35 percent. The maximum drawdown is used by analysts to understand the risk of a particular investment in their portfolio. It is the difference between the top share price and the lowest share price of a company during a particular period.

When looking at Johnson & Johnson and the change in its share price during the recession, it is clear that significant overreaction takes place from investors when the economy is struggling. Despite the entire economy doing so poorly, it does not make sense for investors to abandon stock in companies such as Johnson & Johnson. This is a reliable company that has withstood many poor economic periods in the past, which is highlighted by its incredible success over the past decade.

If investors paid more attention to a company's earnings and dividends, instead of the general market trends, they would not have been in such a rush to sell stock in companies such as Johnson & Johnson.

The Coca-Cola Company (KO) - NYSE			
44.78 ↑0.09(0.20%) May 27, 4:00PM EDT			
Prev Close:	44.69	Day's Range:	44.65 - 44.96
Open:	44.71	52wk Range:	36.56 - 47.13
Bid:	44.81 x 3400	Volume:	7,893,894
Ask:	44.90 x 500	Avg Vol (3m):	13,920,200
1y Target Est:	48.00	Market Cap:	193.73B
Beta:	0.796886	P/E (ttm):	26.96
Earnings Date:	Jul 20 - Jul 25 (Est.)	EPS (ttm):	1.66
		Div & Yield:	1.40 (3.13%)

Figure – Coca-Cola Stock Information
(courtesy Yahoo Finance, 5/27/2016)

The final company in our analysis of the benefits of dividend stocks in economic recessions is Coca-Cola. While the Coca-Cola brand is most often associated with the soft drink of the same name, it is a company that encompasses more than 20 different brands and makes over a billion dollars in sales each year. Brands such as Dasani, Minute Maid, and Gold Peak are part of the Coca-Cola empire.

This is another very consistent company. The earnings-per-share growth over the past ten years is just over seven percent, while dividends increased by nine percent each year in the same time span. Coca-Cola, along with Johnson & Johnson, it is one of the companies that paid dividends to its investors in each of the past 50 years.

Considering Coca-Cola gets most of its business from selling low-cost non-alcoholic drinks, the recession did not have much of an impact on the company's performance. The earnings-per-share was fairly steady from 2007 to 2009, going from $1.29 to $1.51 to $1.47. The small drop from 2008 to 2009 is in contrast to the above two companies, but it is such an insignificant drop that it has no negative impact on an investor or analyst's perception of Coca-Cola.

Chapter 11: Diversification and Changing Markets

The final factor investors must consider when determining the best types of dividend stocks is diversification. In fact, diversification is important any time you are investing in the stock market, whether it is for the purpose of receiving dividends or not.

The idea behind diversification is to lower the risk for the investor. It is impossible to give investors a guarantee that they will never face losses with their stock market investments. No matter how much a person diversifies, they cannot completely eliminate risk. However, most Wall Street analysts believe that the ideal way to minimize investment risk in the long term is with diversification.

Diversification is achieved by purchasing stocks in companies within different sectors, industries, and countries. The goal of diversification is to have a set of stocks in your portfolio where part of the portfolio softens the blow of another part experiencing a bad spell. For example, if you have twenty investments, and five of them have a really bad period, another five investments should rise by a comparable amount to offset the loss from the poorly performing stocks.

Now that you have researched your companies and built a nicely diversified portfolio, it is still important to keep up with market trends.

A major part of having a solid portfolio is stock diversification, and this is only possible when investors keep up with information regarding the companies in their portfolio. Investors must also pay attention to the entire market, and the industries where most of their investments lie. For example, an investor with investments in both a number of technology companies, such as Alphabet (Google) and Apple, must pay attention to market trends that pertain to the technology industry.

By focusing on both companies and their industries, investors can attempt to react before the rest of the market in terms of the stocks they will buy and sell. If an investor is seeing warning signs in the market, they can scale back their investments in certain stocks or industries and reinvest that money elsewhere.

If the overall market trends are predicting a possible recession or period of economic downturn, it makes sense to scale back risky investments and put more of your portfolio into strong dividend paying stocks that guarantee performance every year.

Conclusion

Stocks of companies with a strong history of paying dividends can be an excellent investment. To be successful, you must do your homework on the companies, diversify your funds with different types of companies, and continue to follow the stocks once you have purchased the shares. As the world changes, a once strong company that has paid a great dividend can suffer major setbacks, the stock price will plummet, and the once strong dividend goes away. Stay vigilant and engaged and you will succeed as an investor in dividend paying companies.

Thank you for reading this book. I hope you got a lot of useful information from it. Please don't forget to leave a comment on Amazon. Your honest comments are very helpful and I read every one of them. - Doug

Glossary

2008 Financial Crisis – A global financial crisis that many economists believe was the worst financial crisis since the Great Depression in the 1930s.

Assets – Any resource that has an economic value and is owned by an individual or corporation. Assets are owned with an expectation that they will provide a benefit in the future.

Board of Directors – A group of individuals elected by a company's stockholders. The Board of Directors are tasked with setting goals for a company and making other decisions on behalf of stockholders.

Brokerage – An intermediary business that is primarily tasked with facilitating financial transactions between buyers and sellers. Brokerages earn a commission on each transaction.

Bubble – When the price of a particular stock or market sector rises rapidly, but eventually contracts just as sharply. For example, the United States housing market was experiencing a bubble prior to the 2008 Financial Crisis.

Compound Interest – When interest is not only calculated on the initial principal amount, but also on the accrued interest from past periods. Compound interest provides greater profits over time than regular interest.

Declaration Date – This is the date where the next dividend payment is formally announced by the board of directors of a company. A statement including pertinent information about the dividend is released on the declaration date.

Direct Investment Plans – Plans offered by major companies where investors can bypass brokers and purchase stock directly from the company. These plans make it easier for smaller investors to put their money in a company without having to pay brokerage fees.

Diversification – Investing in assets and commodities from different market sectors in a bid to mitigate against risk in an investment portfolio.

Dividend Aristocrats – A list of all companies that have continued to provide increasing dividends to shareholders over the past 25 years.

Dividend Rate – The dividend rate is a method of calculating the expected dividend payments from a company during a particular period. By multiplying the most recent dividend by the number of dividend periods per year, and adding the extra dividends, you are left with the dividend rate.

Dividend Reinvestment Plans – Plans offered by major companies where investors are able to reinvest the money they earn as dividends back into the company's stock. These plans also offer investors the opportunity to add some of their own money to the dividend payout to buy this stock.

Dividend Yield – A ratio calculation that compares a company's dividend payouts to the share price. The dividend yield is calculated by dividing the annual dividends per share by the price per share.

Dividends – Distribution of funds from the company's earnings to stockholders. The amount and frequency of dividend payments is determined by a company's board of directors.

Earnings – The amount of profit that is produced by a company during a set period of time. When reporting earnings in the financial world, the period of time is typically defined as a quarter, or three months.

Earnings Report – The quarterly earnings report is a filing made by companies to the stock exchange. This earnings report indicates a company's net income, earnings, net sales and earnings per share.

Exchange-Traded Funds – The Exchange-Traded Fund is a security that tracks a particular index, commodity, bond, or set of assets. While comparable to mutual funds, ETFs trade on the stock exchange.

Ex-Dividend Date – This is the date that determines who benefits from the dividend attached to a particular stock. The stock's owner must have bought the stock on or before the ex-dividend date to qualify for the dividend.

Investment Portfolio – Portfolios are typically a group of securities, such as stocks, bonds and other commodities, created with the intention of making a profit for the investor.

Liabilities – Liabilities are legal debt obligations owed by a company through their business operations.

Market Trends – When it comes to the stock market, a trend refers to the direction taken by a particular asset or the entire market. For example, if a company's stock price has steadily risen for the past six months, it is on an upward trend.

Mutual Fund – A mutual fund is a type of investment vehicle where the funds of many investors are collected and used to invest in different financial securities. While mutual funds do charge higher fees than discount brokerages, they are popular because they provide smaller investors with a chance to have their money managed in a professional manner.

Payout Ratio – The payout ratio is method of comparing the earnings a company pays out as dividends to their overall earnings. It is calculated by dividing the dividends per share by the earnings per share.

Price-to-Earnings Ratio – The P/E ratio is used to value a company by measuring the share price in relation to the per-share earnings. By taking the market value per share and dividing it by the earnings per share, we end up with the P/E ratio.

S&P 500 Index – The Standard and Poor's 500 Index is made up of 500 stocks that are chosen based on a number of different factors, such as their market size and liquidity. This index is meant to act as an indicator of how U.S. equities are performing on the market.

Stock Certificate – A piece of paper that provides proof of ownership related to stocks. Most stock certificates are now transferred electronically, which makes trades go through a lot faster than they did in the past.

Stock Exchange – A market where shares of companies are issued, bought and sold on a daily basis. The New York Stock Exchange is the largest and most well-known stock exchange in the world.

Stock Issuance – When a company wants to raise more funds for any reason, they can choose to issue more stocks or shares to the market. The funds they raise from investors buying those stocks will provide them with the necessary capital moving forward.

Stockholders – A stockholder, or shareholder, is someone who owns at least a single share in a particular company's stock.

Stocks - Stocks are securities that typically trade on stock exchanges. The stock security signifies that a person owns a particular percentage of a company, which gives them a claim on part of the company's assets and earnings.

Further Reading

Carlson, C.B. *The Little Book of Big Dividends – A Safe Formula for Guaranteed Returns*. John Wiley & Sons, Inc. 2010.

Hogue, J. *Step By Step Dividend Investing – A Beginner's Guide to the Best Dividend Stocks and Income Investments*. Createspace Publishing. 2015.

Peters, J. *The Ultimate Dividend Playbook – Income, Insight, and Independence for Today's Investor.* John Wiley & Sons, Inc. 2008.

Internet Resources

Website with news and information about dividend paying stocks: http://www.bigsafedividends.com

Website with news and information about dividend paying stocks: http://www.dividend.com

Website with stock information including charts, headlines, price and dividend data: https://finance.yahoo.com

Website with general business and stock news: http://www.bloomberg.com

Disclaimer

The book is for informational purposes only. No investment is without the possibility of loss, including quality dividend paying stocks. Consult your financial advisor before making any investment decisions.

Acknowledgments

I would like to thank Cynthia West, Ansser Sadiq, and Lisa Zahn for their help in preparation of this book.

About the Author

Doug West is a retired engineer, small business owner, and experienced non-fiction writer with several books to his credit. His writing interests are general, with expertise in science, history, biographies, numismatics, and "How To" topics. Doug has a B.S. in Physics from the Missouri School of Science and Technology and a Ph.D. in General Engineering from Oklahoma State University. He lives with his wife and little dog, "Scrappy," near Kansas City, Missouri. Additional books by Doug West can be found at http://www.amazon.com/Doug-West/e/B00961PJ8M. Follow the author on Facebook at: https://www.facebook.com/30minutebooks.

Figure – Doug West (photo by Karina Cinnante)

Additional Books by Doug West

Buying and Selling Silver Bullion Like a Pro

How to Write, Publish and Market Your Own Audio Book

A Short Biography of the Scientist Sir Isaac Newton

A Short Biography of the Astronomer Edwin Hubble

Galileo Galilei – A Short Biography

Benjamin Franklin – A Short Biography

The American Revolutionary War – A Short History

Coinage of the United States – A Short History

John Adams – A Short Biography

In the Footsteps of Columbus (Annotated) Introduction and Biography Included (with Annie J. Cannon)

Alexander Hamilton – Illustrated and Annotated (with Charles A. Conant)

Harlow Shapley – Biography of an Astronomer

Alexander Hamilton – A Short Biography

The Great Depression – A Short History

Jesse Owens, Adolf Hitler and the 1936 Summer Olympics

Thomas Jefferson – A Short Biography

Gold of My Father – A Short Tale of Adventure

Index

A

Apple 4, 29, 50
Assets 53

B

brokerage viii, 2, 7, 54

C

Clorox 44, 45
Coca-Cola 36, 47, 48

D

declaration date 17, 54
dividend v, vii, 3, 16, 17, 18, 19, 21, 22, 23, 25, 26, 27, 29, 31, 32,
 33, 35, 36, 39, 40, 41, 43, 44, 47, 49, 50, 51, 54, 55, 56, 60, 61
Dividend Rate 18, 19, 54
Dividend Reinvestment Plan 22
Dividend Reinvestment Programs 22, 25

E

ETF 16
eTrade 8
Exchange-Traded Fund
 ETF 55

G

General Motors 30

J

Johnson & Johnson 45, 46, 48

L

Loyal3 8

M

Merrill Edge 8
Microsoft 4, 29

O

OptionsHouse 8

P

payout ratio 18, 20, 29, 30, 31, 32, 33, 56
P/E ratio 31, 32, 33, 57
price-to-earnings 31

R

Robinhood 8

S

shareholders 1, 2, 3, 4, 15, 16, 17, 20, 54
stock certificate 1
stock market viii, ix, 5, 6, 7, 9, 12, 13, 26, 27, 49, 56
stock price 3, 4, 6, 10, 11, 12, 13, 27, 32, 33, 36, 39, 40, 51, 56

V

Verizon Communications 30, 32